Meditate On This

An aide to meditating upon and memorizing sound doctrine

©2015 by Dean Isaacson

ISBN: 978-0-578-17253-8

Published by cominus

PO Box 178 Hayden ID 83835

All Scripture based upon the ESV Version but is not always an exact or true copy. The author has taken the liberty to capitalize divine pronouns and has made adjustments to punctuation, grammar and, in a few cases, minor wording changes for clarification.

The Holy Bible, English Standard Version® (ESV®) Copyright © 2001 by Crossway, a publishing ministry of Good News Publishers. All rights reserved. ESV Text Edition: 2007

Introduction

The Apostle Paul warned us to examine ourselves to see if we are in the faith (2Co 13:5). Most of us just read past this verse and think if we are sincere in our faith, then our faith is real. We convince ourselves we love God and we may even feel it emotionally. Yet, the Apostle John told us if we love God we will keep His commands (1Jo 2:3) and Jesus asked why we call Him "Lord" but do not obey Him (Luk 6:46). We deceive ourselves if we believe sincerity overcomes doctrine.

We see the few professing Christians who stand boldly for the truth of God's Word are rebuked and disowned by the many professing Christians who want the Gospel to appeal to the masses. The ones who stand for truth are labeled as divisive; yet the real division in the body of Christ comes from using worldly wisdom to syncretize the faith - to appeal to the unsaved world (see 1Co 2:6). We ignore Christ's claim He intended to bring division in the world (Mat 10:34; Luk 12:51).

Most professing American Christians follow doctrine which makes them feel comfortable and do not realize this is the "itching ears" syndrome the Apostle Paul warned about (2Ti 4:3). We say we believe God is sovereign but we cling desperately to any and all sovereignty of our own - especially the falsely understood sovereignty of freewill (see Jer 17:9). If our doctrine is self-centered or self-improvement centered, it is not God-centered.

As a body of professing believers, we are not in the Word and few are committed to memorizing the Scriptures. Yet, among those who do, most of this memorization is focused on God's promises which we have taken out of context. Once again, this reflects our self-centered faith.

Memory of Scripture should lead to sound doctrine but this is subject to how we select our favorite verses. The Scriptures we choose to memorize should reflect a faith focused on glorifying God alone. Joshua 1:8 says this Book of the Law shall not depart from your mouth. . . meditate on this. . .

We think we are in the faith but so often fail to examine ourselves according to the Scriptures. So, let us take the Apostle Paul's warning seriously to examine ourselves. He wrote much about following sound doctrine.

Meditate On This is an aid to memorizing and meditating upon sound doctrine. Review the verses in this book over-and-over - memorize them - and allow the Holy Spirit to speak to you. May your walk with Christ exalt God alone.

Hopefully, this book will not be the end of your efforts to memorize God's Word - may it be the beginning or a new beginning.

There are two articles after the verse section designed to help you look at modern theological claims through the Scripture. Hopefully, you will develop critical thinking based upon Scripture, rather than commonly-held platitudes and extra-Biblical theories and theology.

The first article, *Not Willing Any Should Perish* (pg 61), looks at the claims God wants all men to be saved and that one is saved by saying the sinner's prayer, if at least to have fire insurance.

The second article, *Freewill vs John 3:16* (pg 91), looks at the claims Christ died for the whole world and whether we are saved by our own choice or God's will.

If you find you do not agree with me, search the Scriptures to see what they say. May your conclusions reflect the Word of Truth even if they conflict with what you were taught. Most of us, in modern American churches, have been taught wrong.

Keep the faith.

"In the beginning, God created the heavens and the earth." Gen 1:1

"I will put enmity between you and the woman and between your offspring and her offspring; He shall bruise your head and you shall bruise His heel." Gen 3:15

". . . For the intention of man's heart is evil from his youth." Gen 8:21

". . . Look for able men from all the people, men who fear God, who are trustworthy and hate a bribe and place such men over the people. . ." Exo 18:21

". . . Please show me Your ways, so I may know You and find favor in Your sight. . ." Exo 33:13

". . . I will be gracious to whom I will be gracious and will show mercy on whom I will show mercy." Exo 33:19

"God is not man, so that He should lie, or a son of man, so that He should change his mind. . ." Num 23:19

". . . Gather the people to Me, so that I may let them hear My words, so that they may learn to fear Me all the days they live on the earth and they may teach their children so." Deu 4:10

"He is your praise. He is your God. . ." Deu 10:21

"The secret things belong to the Lord our God, but the things revealed belong to us and to our children forever, so that we may do all the words of this law." Deu 29:29

"This Book of the Law shall not depart from your mouth, but you shall meditate on it day and night, so that you may be careful to do according to everything written in it. For then you will make your way prosperous and then you will have good success." Jos 1:8

"For it was the Lord's doing to harden their hearts that they should come against Israel in battle, in order that they should be devoted to destruction and should receive no mercy. . ." Jos 11:20

"Now therefore fear the Lord and serve Him in sincerity and in faithfulness. Put away [your idols] and serve the Lord." Jos 24:14

". . . Far be it from me that I should sin against the Lord by ceasing to pray for you. . ." 1Sa 1:23

". . . The Glory of Israel will not lie or have regret, for He is not a man, that He should have regret." 1Sa 15:29

"He trains my hands for war. . ." 2Sa 22:35

". . . There is no God like You, in heaven above or on earth beneath, keeping covenant and showing steadfast love to Your servants who walk before You with all their heart." 1Ki 8:23

"So these nations feared the Lord and also served their carved images. . ." 2Ki 17:41

". . . Yours, O Lord, is the greatness and the power and the glory and the victory and the majesty, for all that is in the heavens and in the earth is Yours. Yours is the kingdom, O Lord and You are exalted as head above all." 1Ch 29:11

". . . O Lord, there is none like You to help between the mighty and the weak. Help us, O Lord our God, for we rely on You. . ." 2Ch 14:11

". . . Blessed be Your glorious name, which is exalted above all blessing and praise. You are the Lord, You alone. You have made heaven, the highest heavens, with all their host, the earth and all that is on it, the seas and all that is in them; and You preserve all of them; and the host of heaven worships You." Neh 9:5-6

"For affliction does not come from the dust nor does trouble sprout from the ground." Job 5:6

"Who can bring a clean thing out of an unclean?" Job 14:4

". . . Behold, the fear of the Lord is wisdom and to turn away from evil is understanding." Job 28:28

"I know You can do all things and no purpose of Yours can be thwarted." Job 42:2

"Blessed is the man who walks not in the counsel of the wicked nor stands in the way of sinners nor sits in the seat of scoffers; but his delight is in the law of the Lord and on His law he meditates day and night." Psa 1:1-2

". . . Be warned, O rulers of the earth. Serve the Lord with fear and rejoice with trembling." Psa 2:10-11

"O Lord, in the morning You hear my voice; in the morning I prepare a sacrifice for You and watch." Psa 5:3

"The counsel of the Lord stands forever, the plans of his heart to all generations." Psa 33:11

"For the Lord loves justice; He will not forsake His saints. They are preserved forever. . ." Psa 37:28

"Behold, I was brought forth in iniquity and in sin did my mother conceive me." Psa 51:5

"When I am afraid, I put my trust in You. In God, whose word I praise, in God I trust; I shall not be afraid. . ." Psa 56:3-4

"I cry out to God Most High, to God who fulfills His purpose for me." Psa 57:2

"The wicked are estranged from the womb; they go astray from birth. . ." Psa 58:3

"Blessed is the one You choose and bring near, to dwell in Your courts. . ." Psa 65:4

"Say to God, 'How awesome are Your deeds! So great is Your power Your enemies come cringing to You. All the earth worships You and sings praises to You'. . ." Psa 66:3-4

"Who will rise up for Me against the wicked? Who will stand up for Me against the evildoers?" Psa 94:16

"He does not deal with us according to our sins nor repay us according to our iniquities. For as high as the heavens are above the earth, so great is His steadfast love toward those who fear Him." Psa 103:10-11

"I will give thanks to You, O Lord, among the peoples; I will sing praises to You among the nations. For Your steadfast love is great above the heavens; Your faithfulness reaches to the clouds. Be exalted, O God, above the heavens! Let Your glory be over all the earth." Psa 108:3-5

"Your people will offer themselves freely on the day of Your power. . ." Psa 110:3

"Our God is in the heavens; He does all He pleases." Psa 115:3

"It is better to take refuge in the Lord than to trust in man." Psa 118:8

"Your word is a lamp to my feet and a light to my path." Psa 119:105

"Long have I known from Your testimonies You have founded them forever." Psa 119:152

"Pray for the peace of Jerusalem. . ." Psa 122:6

"I give You thanks, O Lord, with my whole heart; before the gods I sing Your praise . . . for You have exalted above all things Your name and Your word." Psa 138;1-2

"The Lord will fulfill His purpose for me; Your steadfast love, O Lord, endures forever." Psa 138:8

". . . You wrote in Your book all my days before one of them came to be." Psa 139:16

"The fear of the Lord is the beginning of knowledge. . ." Pro 1:7

"Trust in the Lord with all your heart and do not lean on your own understanding. In all your ways acknowledge Him and He will make straight your paths." Pro 3:5-6

"Righteousness exalts a nation, but sin is a reproach to any people." Pro 14:34

"The plans of the heart belong to man, but the answer of the tongue is from the Lord." Pro 16:1

"The Lord has made everything for His purpose, even the wicked for the day of trouble." Pro 16:4

"The heart of man plans his way, but the Lord directs his steps." Pro 16:9

"The lot is cast into the lap, but its every decision is from the Lord." Pro 16:33

"Whoever is generous to the poor lends to the Lord. . ." Pro 19:17

"Many are the plans in the mind of a man, but it is the purpose of the Lord that will stand." Pro 19:21

"Who can say, 'I have made my heart pure; I am clean from my sin.'" Pro 20:9

"The king's heart is a stream of water in the hand of the Lord; He turns it wherever He will." Pro 21:1

"The horse is made ready for the day of battle, but the victory belongs to the Lord." Pro 21:31

"Rescue those being lead away to death; hold back those stumbling to the slaughter. If you say, 'Behold, we did not know this,' does not He who weighs the heart perceive it. . ." Pro 24:11-12

"Those who forsake the law praise the wicked, but those who keep the law strive against them. Evil men do not understand justice, but those who seek the Lord understand it completely." Pro 28:4-5

"Open your mouth for the mute, for the rights of all who are destitute. . . defend the rights of the poor and needy." Pro 31:8-9

"In the day of prosperity be joyful and in the day of adversity consider: God has made the one as well as the other, so that man may not find out anything that will be after him." Ecc 7:14

". . . There is no discharge from war nor will wickedness deliver those given to it." Ecc 8:8

"Because the sentence against an evil deed is not executed speedily, the heart of the children of man is fully set to do evil." Ecc 8:11

"A wise man's heart inclines him to the right, but a fool's heart to the left." Ecc 10:2

". . . Fear God and keep His commandments, for this is the whole duty of man." Ecc 12:13

". . . The Lord alone will be exalted in that day." Isa 2:11

"Woe to those who call evil good and good evil. . ." Isa 5:20

". . . Holy, holy, holy is the Lord of hosts; the whole earth is full of his glory." Isa 6:3

"Do not call conspiracy what this people calls conspiracy and do not fear what they fear nor be in dread. But the Lord of hosts, Him you shall honor as holy. Let Him be your fear and let Him be your dread." Isa 8:12-13

". . . As I have planned, so shall it be. . ." Isa 14:24

"O Lord, You are my God; I will exalt You; I will praise Your name, for You have done wonderful things, plans formed of old, faithful and sure." Isa 25:1

". . . For You have done for us all our works." Isa 26:12

"O Lord, be gracious to us; we wait for You. Be our strength every morning, our salvation in the time of trouble." Isa 33:2

". . . I am God and there is none like Me . . . My counsel shall stand and I will accomplish all My purpose." Isa 46:9-10

". . . He bore the sin of many and makes intercession for transgressors." Isa 53:12

"For My thoughts are not your thoughts, neither are your ways My ways, declares the Lord." Isa 55:8

"So shall My word be that goes out from My mouth; it shall not return to Me empty, but it shall accomplish what I purpose. . ." Isa 55:11

"You who put the Lord in remembrance, take no rest, and give Him no rest until He establishes Jerusalem and makes it a praise in the earth." Isa 62:6-7

". . . We are the clay and You are the potter; we are all the work of Your hand." Isa 64:8

"Do not trust in these deceptive words:'This is the temple of the Lord, the temple of the Lord, the temple of the Lord.'" Jer 7:4

"I know, O Lord, the way of man is not in himself, it is not in man who walks to direct his steps. Correct me, O Lord, but in justice; not in Your anger, lest You bring me to nothing." Jer 10:23-24

"The heart is deceitful above all things and desperately wicked; who can understand it." Jer 17:9

"Ah, Lord God! It is You who have made the heavens and the earth by Your great power and by Your outstretched arm! Nothing is too hard for You." Jer 32:17

"Call to Me and I will answer you and will tell you great and hidden things you have not known." Jer 33:3

"Who has spoken and it came to pass, unless the Lord has commanded it." Lam 3:37

"Is it not from the mouth of the Most High that good and bad come." Lam 3:38

"You, O Lord, reign forever; Your throne endures to all generations." Lam 5:19

"Restore us to yourself, O Lord, that we may be restored! Renew our days as of old - unless You have utterly rejected us. . ." Lam 5:21-22

"And I will give you a new heart and a new spirit I will put within you. And I will remove the heart of stone and give you a heart of flesh. And I will put My Spirit within you and cause you to walk in My statutes and be careful to obey My rules." Eze 36:26-27

". . . Blessed be the name of God forever and ever, to whom belong wisdom and might. He changes times and seasons; He removes kings and sets up kings; He gives wisdom to the wise and knowledge to those who have understanding." Dan 2:20-21

"All the inhabitants of the earth are accounted as nothing and He does according to His will among the host of heaven and among the inhabitants of the earth; and none can stay His hand or say to him, 'What have you done?'" Dan 4:35

". . . For we do not present our pleas before You because of our righteousness, but because of Your great mercy." Dan 9:18

"My people are destroyed for lack of knowledge. . ." Hos 4:6

"They made kings but not through Me." Hos 8:4

". . . The ways of the Lord are right and the upright walk in them but transgressors stumble in them." Hos 14:9

". . . Everyone who calls on the name of the Lord shall be saved." Joe 2:32

". . . Does disaster come to a city, unless the Lord has done it?" Amo 3:6

"For the day of the Lord is near upon all the nations. As you have done, it shall be done to you; your deeds shall return on your own head." Oba 1:15

". . . Salvation belongs to the Lord." Jon 2:9

"He has told you, O man, what is good; and what does the Lord require of you but to do justice and to love mercy and to walk humbly with your God?" Mic 6:8

"The righteous will live by his faith." Hab 2:4

"O Lord, I have heard the report of You and Your work, O Lord, do I fear. In the midst of the years revive it; in the midst of the years make it known; in wrath remember mercy." Hab 3:2

". . . Not by might nor by power, but by my Spirit, says the Lord of hosts." Zec 4:6

"For I the Lord do not change. . ." Mal 3:6

"She will bear a son and you shall call his name Jesus, for He will save His people from their sins." Mat 1:21

"[Jesus said] Repent, for the kingdom of heaven is at hand." Mat 4:17

"Do not lay up for yourselves treasures on earth, where moth and rust destroy and where thieves break in and steal, but lay up for yourselves treasures in heaven, where neither moth nor rust destroys and where thieves do not break in and steal. For where your treasure is, there your heart will be also." Mat 6:19-21

". . . If then the light in you is darkness, how great is the darkness." Mat 6:23

"But seek first the kingdom of God and His righteousness and all these things will be added to you. Therefore do not be anxious about tomorrow, for tomorrow will be anxious for itself. Sufficient for the day is its own trouble." Mat 6:33-34

"Not everyone who says to me, 'Lord, Lord,' will enter the kingdom of heaven, but the one who does the will of My Father. . ." Mat 7:21

". . . I have not come to bring peace, but a sword." Mat 10:34

"From the days of John the Baptist until now the kingdom of heaven has been forcefully advancing and forceful men lay hold of it." Mat 11:12

". . . No one knows the Son except the Father and no one knows the Father except the Son and anyone to whom the Son chooses to reveal Him." Mat 11:27

". . . For it is necessary that temptations come, but woe to the one by whom the temptation comes!" Mat 18:7

". . . 'Truly, I say to you, only with difficulty will a rich person enter the kingdom of heaven' . . . When the disciples heard this, they were greatly astonished, saying, 'Who then can be saved?' But Jesus looked at them and said, 'With man this is impossible, but with God all things are possible.'" Mat 19:23-26

". . . The Son of Man came not to be served but to serve, and to give His life as a ransom for many." Mat 20:28

"For many are called, but few are chosen." Mat 22:14

"For this is My blood of the covenant, which is poured out for many for the forgiveness of sins." Mat 26:28

". . . All authority in heaven and on earth has been given to Me. Go therefore and make disciples of all nations, baptizing them in the name of the Father and of the Son and of the Holy Spirit, teaching them to observe all I have commanded you. And behold, I am with you always, to the end of the age." Mat 28:18-20

". . . No one is good except God alone. . ." Mar 10:18

"Why do you call Me 'Lord, Lord' and not do what I tell you." Luk 6:46

"I thank You, Father, Lord of heaven and earth, You have hidden these things from the wise and revealed them to little children." Luk 10:21

"Do you think that I have come to give peace on earth? No, I tell you, but rather division." Luk 12:51

"But to all who did receive Him, who believed in His name, He gave the right to become children of God, who were born, not of blood nor of the will of the flesh nor of the will of man, but of God." Joh 1:12-13

". . . Unless one is born again he cannot see the kingdom of God." Joh 3:3

"And this is the judgment: the light has come into the world and people loved the darkness rather than the light because their deeds were evil." Joh 3:19

"Whoever believes in the Son has eternal life; whoever does not obey the Son shall not see life, but the wrath of God remains on him." Joh 3:36

"For as the Father raises the dead and gives them life, so also the Son gives life to whom He will." Joh 5:21

"How can you believe, when you receive glory from one another and do not seek the glory that comes from the only God?" Joh 5:44

". . . This is the work of God, that you believe in Him whom He has sent." Joh 6:29

"All the Father gives Me will come to Me and whoever comes to Me I will never cast out." Joh 6:37

"No one can come to Me unless the Father who sent Me draws him. . ." Joh 6:44

"It is the Spirit who gives life; the flesh is no help at all. . ." Joh 6:63

". . . No one can come to Me unless it is granted him by the Father." Joh 6:65

"If you abide in My word, you are truly My disciples and you will know the truth and the truth will set you free." Joh 8:31-32

"But you do not believe because you are not my sheep." Joh 10:26

"My sheep hear My voice and I know them and they follow Me." Joh 10:27

"I give them eternal life and they will never perish and no one will snatch them out of My hand. My Father, who has given them to Me, is greater than all and no one is able to snatch them out of the Father's hand." Joh 10:28-29

"He has blinded their eyes and hardened their heart, lest they see with their eyes and understand with their heart and turn and I would heal them." Joh 12:40

". . . I know whom I have chosen. . ." Joh 13:18

". . . I am the way, the truth and the life. No one comes to the Father except through Me." Joh 14:6

"I am the true vine and My Father is the vinedresser. Every branch in Me that does not bear fruit He takes away and every branch that does bear fruit He prunes, that it may bear more fruit." Joh 15:1-2

"I am the vine; you are the branches. Whoever abides in Me and I in him, he it is that bears much fruit, for apart from Me you can do nothing. If anyone does not abide in Me he is thrown away like a branch and withers; and the branches are gathered, thrown into the fire and burned." Joh 15:5-6

"You did not choose Me, but I chose you. . ." Joh 15:16

". . . I am not praying for the world but for those whom You have given Me, for they are Yours." Joh 17:9

"Father, I desire they also, whom You have given Me, may be with Me where I am, to see My glory You have given Me because you loved Me before the foundation of the world." Joh 17:24

"There is salvation in no one else, for there is no other name under heaven given among men by which we must be saved." Act 4:12

". . . As many as were appointed to eternal life believed." Act 13:48

"One who heard us was a woman named Lydia . . . The Lord opened her heart to pay attention to what was said by Paul." Act 16:14

"And He made from one man every nation of mankind to live on all the face of the earth, having determined allotted periods and the boundaries of their dwelling place." Act 17:26

"The times of ignorance God overlooked, but now He commands all people everywhere to repent." Act 17:30

"He has fixed a day on which He will judge the world in righteousness by a man whom He has appointed; and of this He has given assurance to all by raising Him from the dead." Act 17:31

". . . From among your own selves will arise men speaking twisted things, to draw away the disciples after them." Act 20:30

"For I am not ashamed of the gospel, for it is the power of God for salvation to everyone who believes. . ." Rom 1:16

"For His invisible attributes, namely, His eternal power and divine nature, have been clearly perceived, ever since the creation of the world, in the things that have been made. So they are without excuse." Rom 1:20

"For although they knew God, they did not honor Him as God or give thanks to Him, but they became futile in their thinking and their foolish hearts were darkened. Claiming to be wise, they became fools." Rom 1:21-22

"Therefore God gave them up in the lusts of their hearts to impurity, to the dishonoring of their bodies among themselves, because they exchanged the truth about God for a lie and worshiped and served the creature rather than the Creator, who is blessed forever! Amen." Rom 1:24-25

". . . No one is righteous. . . no one understands; no one seeks after God." Rom 3:10-12

"For all have sinned and fall short of the glory of God." Rom 3:23

"Therefore, since we have been justified by faith, we have peace with God through our Lord Jesus Christ." Rom 5:1

". . . While we were enemies we were reconciled to God by the death of His Son. . ." Rom 5:10

". . . Sin came into the world through one man and death through sin and so death spread to all men because all sinned." Rom 5:12

"What shall we say then? Are we to continue in sin so that grace may abound? By no means! How can we who died to sin still live in it." Rom 6:1-2

"What then? Are we to sin because we are not under law but under grace? By no means! Do you not know . . . you are slaves of the one whom you obey. . ." Rom 6:15-16

"For the wages of sin is death, but the free gift of God is eternal life in Christ Jesus our Lord." Rom 6:23

"For the mind set on the flesh is hostile to God, for it does not submit to God's law; indeed, it cannot." Rom 8:7

"Those in the flesh cannot please God." Rom 8:8

"For all led by the Spirit of God are sons of God." Rom 8:14

"For I consider the sufferings of this present time are not worth comparing with the glory that is to be revealed to us." Rom 8:18

"Likewise the Spirit helps us in our weakness. For we do not know what to pray for as we ought, but the Spirit Himself intercedes for us with groanings too deep for words. And He who searches hearts knows what is the mind of the Spirit, because the Spirit intercedes for the saints according to the will of God." Rom 8:26-27

"And we know for those who love God all things work together for good, for those who are called according to His purpose." Rom 8:28

"For those whom He foreknew He also predestined to be conformed to the image of His Son, in order that He might be the firstborn among many brothers. And those whom He predestined He also called and those whom He called he also justified and those whom He justified He also glorified." Rom 8:29-30

"No, in all these things we are more than conquerors through Him who loved us. For I am sure neither death nor life nor angels nor rulers nor things present nor things to come nor powers nor height nor depth nor anything else in all creation, will be able to separate us from the love of God in Christ Jesus our Lord." Rom 8:37-39

"Though they were not yet born and had done nothing either good or bad - in order that God's purpose of election might continue, not because of works but because of Him who calls— she was told, 'The older will serve the younger.' As it is written, 'Jacob I loved, but Esau I hated.'" Rom 9:11-13

"What shall we say then? Is there injustice on God's part? By no means! For He said to Moses, 'I will have mercy on whom I have mercy and I will have compassion on whom I have compassion.' So then it depends not on human will or exertion, but on God, who has mercy." Rom 9:14-16

"So then He has mercy on whomever He wills and He hardens whomever He wills." Rom 9:18

"You will say to me then, 'Why does He still find fault? For who can resist His will?' But who are you, O man, to answer back to God? Will what is molded say to its molder, 'Why have you made me like this?'" Rom 9:19-20

"What if God, desiring to show His wrath and to make known His power, has endured with much patience vessels of wrath prepared for destruction, in order to make known the riches of His glory for vessels of mercy, which he has prepared beforehand for glory - even us whom He has called? . . ." Rom 9:22-24

"Behold, I am laying in Zion a stone of stumbling and a rock of offense; and whoever believes in Him will not be put to shame." Rom 9:33

"If you confess with your mouth Jesus is Lord and believe in your heart God raised Him from the dead, you will be saved. For with the heart one believes and is justified and with the mouth one confesses and is saved." Rom 10:9-10

"Oh, the depth of the riches and wisdom and knowledge of God! How unsearchable are His judgments and how inscrutable His ways! For who has known the mind of the Lord, or who has been His counselor?" Rom 11:33-34

"For from Him and through Him and to Him are all things. To Him be glory forever. Amen." Rom 11:36

". . . Present your bodies as a living sacrifice, holy and acceptable to God, which is your spiritual worship. Do not be conformed to this world, but be transformed by the renewal of your mind. So that by testing you may discern what is the will of God, what is good, acceptable and perfect." Rom 12:1-2

"The God of peace will soon crush Satan under your feet. . ." Rom 16:20

"Who will sustain you to the end, guiltless in the day of our Lord Jesus Christ. God is faithful, by whom you were called into the fellowship of His Son, Jesus Christ our Lord." 1Co 1:8-9

"For consider your calling, brothers: not many of you were wise according to worldly standards, not many were powerful, not many were of noble birth. But God chose what is foolish in the world to shame the wise; God chose what is weak in the world to shame the strong; God chose what is low and despised in the world . . . so that no human being might boast in the presence of God. And because of him you are in Christ Jesus . . . so that, as it is written, 'Let the one who boasts, boast in the Lord.'" 1Co 1:26-31

". . . It is not a wisdom of this age or of the rulers of this age, who are doomed to pass away." 1Co 2:6

"The natural person does not accept the things of the Spirit of God, for they are folly to him and he is not able to understand them because they are spiritually discerned." 1Co 2:14

"Let no one deceive himself. If anyone among you thinks he is wise in this age, let him become a fool so that he may become wise. For the wisdom of this world is folly with God. . ." 1Co 3:18-19

". . . What do you have that you did not receive? If then you received it, why do you boast as if you did not receive it?" 1Co 4:7

"Do you not know that your body is a temple of the Holy Spirit within you, whom you have from God? You are not your own, for you were bought with a price. So glorify God in your body." 1Co 6:19-20

". . . Do all to the glory of God." 1Co 10:31

". . . There must be factions among you in order that those who are genuine among you may be recognized." 1Co 11:19

"This is why many of you are weak and ill and some have died. But if we judged ourselves rightly, we would be spared this judgment. But when we are judged by the Lord, we are disciplined so that we may not be condemned along with the world." 1Co 11:30-32

"For we must all appear before the judgment seat of Christ, so that each one may receive what is due for what he has done in the body, whether good or evil." 2Co 5:10

". . . If anyone is in Christ, he is a new creation. The old has passed away. . ." 2Co 5:17

"We destroy arguments and every lofty opinion raised against the knowledge of God and take every thought captive to obey Christ." 2Co 10:5

"Examine yourselves, to see whether you are in the faith. . ." 2Co 13:5

"Grace to you and peace from God our Father and the Lord Jesus Christ, who gave Himself for our sins to deliver us from the present evil age, according to the will of our God and Father." Gal 1:3-4

"Christ redeemed us from the curse of the law by becoming a curse for us - for it is written, 'Cursed is everyone who is hanged on a tree.'" Gal 3:13

"The fruit of the Spirit is love, joy, peace, patience, kindness, goodness, faithfulness, gentleness, self- control; against such things there is no law." Gal 5:22

". . . He chose us in Him before the foundation of the world. . . In love He predestined us for adoption as sons through Jesus Christ, according to the purpose of His will." Eph 1:4-5

"In Him we have obtained an inheritance, having been predestined according to the purpose of Him who works all things according to the counsel of His will." Eph 1:11

". . . The God of our Lord Jesus Christ, the Father of glory, may give you the Spirit of wisdom and of revelation in the knowledge of him, having the eyes of your hearts enlightened, so that you may know what is the hope to which He has called you. . ." Eph 1:17-18

"And you were dead in the trespasses and sins in which you once walked, following the course of this world, following the prince of the power of the air, the spirit that is now at work in the sons of disobedience - among whom we all once lived in the passions of our flesh, carrying out the desires of the body and the mind. . ." Eph 2:1-3

"But God, being rich in mercy, because of the great love with which He loved us, even when we were dead in our trespasses, made us alive together with Christ. . ." Eph 2:4-5

"For by grace you have been saved through faith. And this is not your own doing; it is the gift of God, not a result of works, so that no one may boast." Eph 2:8-9

"For we are His workmanship, created in Christ Jesus for good works, which God prepared beforehand, so that we should walk in them." Eph 2:10

"For at one time you were darkness, but now you are light in the Lord." Eph 5:8

"Husbands, love your wives, as Christ loved the church and gave Himself up for her." Eph 5:25

". . . He who began a good work in you will bring it to completion at the day of Jesus Christ." Php 1:6

". . . At the name of Jesus every knee shall bow, in heaven and on earth and under the earth and every tongue confess Jesus Christ is Lord, to the glory of God the Father." Php 2:10-11

". . . Work out your own salvation with fear and trembling, for it is God who works in you, both to will and to work for His good pleasure." Php 2:12-13

"Rejoice in the Lord always. . ." Php 4:4

"Do not be anxious about anything, but in everything by prayer and supplication with thanksgiving let your requests be made known to God." Php 4:6

". . . Whatever is true, whatever is honorable, whatever is just, whatever is pure, whatever is lovely, whatever is commendable, if there is any excellence, if there is anything worthy of praise, think about these things." Php 4:8

"He has delivered us from the domain of darkness and transferred us to the kingdom of His beloved Son, in whom we have redemption, the forgiveness of sins." Col 1:13-14

"For by Him all things were created, in heaven and on earth, visible and invisible, whether thrones or dominions or rulers or authorities - all things were created through Him and for Him." Col 1:16

"Therefore, as you received Christ Jesus the Lord, so walk in Him, rooted and built up in Him and established in the faith, just as you were taught, abounding in thanksgiving." Col 2:6-7

"See to it no one takes you captive by philosophy and empty deceit, according to human tradition, according to the elemental spirits of the world and not according to Christ." Col 2:8

"For in Him the whole fullness of deity dwells bodily." Col 2:9

"And whatever you do, in word or deed, do everything in the name of the Lord Jesus, giving thanks to God the Father through Him." Col 3:17

"Continue steadfastly in prayer, being watchful in it with thanksgiving." Col 4:2

"For we know, brothers loved by God, He has chosen you." 1Th 1:4

"Rejoice always, pray without ceasing, give thanks in all circumstances; for this is the will of God in Christ Jesus for you." 1Th 5:16-18

"He who calls you is faithful; He will surely do it." 1Th 5:24

". . . God chose you as the firstfruits to be saved, through sanctification by the Spirit and belief in the truth." 2Th 2:13

"Keep a close watch on yourself and on the teaching. Persist in this, for by so doing you will save both yourself and your hearers." 1Ti 4:16

"Who saved us and called us to a holy calling, not because of our works but because of His own purpose and grace, which He gave us in Christ Jesus before the ages began." 2Ti 1:9

". . . But I am not ashamed, for I know whom I have believed and I am convinced He is able to guard until the Day what has been entrusted to me." 2Ti 1:12

"Do your best to present yourself to God as one approved, a worker who has no need to be ashamed, rightly handling the word of truth." 2Ti 2:15

"Correcting His opponents with gentleness. God may perhaps grant them repentance leading to a knowledge of the truth and they may come to their senses and escape from the snare of the devil, after being captured by him to do his will." 2Ti 2:25-26

"All who desire to live a godly life in Christ Jesus will be persecuted, while evil people and impostors will go on from bad to worse, deceiving and being deceived." 2Ti 3:12-13

"All Scripture is breathed out by God and profitable for teaching, for reproof, for correction and for training in righteousness, so that the man of God may be complete, equipped for every good work." 2Ti 3:16-17

"For the time is coming when people will not endure sound doctrine, but having itching ears they will accumulate for themselves teachers to suit their own passions." 2Ti 4:3

"They profess to know God, but they deny Him by their works." Tit 1:16

". . . Teach what accords with sound doctrine." Tit 2:1

"He saved us, not because of works done by us in righteousness, but according to His own mercy. . ." Tit 3:5

". . . He upholds the universe by the word of His power. . ." Heb 1:3

"For every house is built by someone, but the builder of all things is God." Heb 3:4

"For the word of God is living and active, sharper than any two-edged sword, piercing to the division of soul and of spirit, of joints and of marrow and discerning the thoughts and intentions of the heart." Heb 4:12

"Therefore He is the mediator of a new covenant, so that those who are called may receive the promised eternal inheritance. . ." Heb 9:15

". . . Without the shedding of blood there is no forgiveness of sins." Heb 9:22

". . . It is appointed for man to die once and after this comes judgment." Heb 9:27

"Now faith is the assurance of things hoped for, the conviction of things not seen." Heb 11:1

"Without faith it is impossible to please Him, for whoever would draw near to God must believe He exists and He rewards those who seek Him." Heb 11:6

"Therefore, since we are surrounded by so great a cloud of witnesses, let us lay aside every weight and sin which clings so closely and let us run with endurance the race set before us." Heb 12:1

"Jesus Christ is the same yesterday, today and forever." Heb 13:8

"If any of you lacks wisdom, let him ask God, who gives generously to all without reproach. . ." Jam 1:5

"Let no one say when he is tempted, 'I am being tempted by God,' for God cannot be tempted with evil and He Himself tempts no one." Jam 1:13

"Of His own will He brought us forth by the word of truth. . ." Jam 1:18

"But be doers of the word and not hearers only, deceiving yourselves." Jam 1:22

"What good is it, my brothers, if someone says he has faith but does not have works? Can that faith save him." Jam 2:14

"You believe that God is one; you do well. Even the demons believe - and shudder." Jam 2:19

"Was not Abraham our father justified by works when he offered up his son Isaac on the altar? You see that faith was active along with his works and faith was completed by his works; and the Scripture was fulfilled that says, 'Abraham believed God and it was counted to him as righteousness'. . ." Jam 2:21-23

". . . Do you not know that friendship with the world is enmity with God? . . ." Jam 4:4

"Submit yourselves therefore to God. Resist the devil and he will flee from you." Jam 4:7

". . . What is your life? For you are a mist that appears for a little time and then vanishes." Jam 4:14

"Do not grumble against one another, brothers, so that you may not be judged; behold, the Judge is standing at the door." Jam 5:9

". . .Those who are elect . . . according to the foreknowledge of God the Father, in the sanctification of the Spirit, for obedience to Jesus Christ." 1Pe 1:1-2

". . . According to His great mercy, He has caused us to be born again. . ." 1Pe 1:3

"You have been born again, not of perishable seed but of imperishable, through the living and abiding word of God." 1Pe 1:23

"But you are a chosen race, a royal priesthood, a holy nation, a people for His own possession, so that you may proclaim the excellencies of Him who called you out of darkness into His marvelous light." 1Pe 2:9

"He Himself bore our sins in His body on the tree, so that we might die to sin and live to righteousness." 1Pe 2:24

"For the eyes of the Lord are on the righteous and His ears are open to their prayer. . ." 1Pe 3:12

". . . Always be prepared to make a defense to anyone who asks you for a reason for the hope in you; yet do it with gentleness and respect." 1Pe 3:15

"The end of all things is at hand; therefore be self-controlled and sober-minded for the sake of your prayers." 1Pe 4:7

"Casting all your anxieties on Him, because He cares for you." 1Pe 5:7

"They promise them freedom, but they themselves are slaves of corruption." 2Pe 2:19

"The Lord is not slow to fulfill His promise as some count slowness, but is patient toward you, not wishing any should perish, but all should reach repentance." 2Pe 3:9

". . . Take care that you are not carried away with the teachings of lawless people . . ." 2Pe 3:17

"If we say we have no sin, we deceive ourselves and the truth is not in us. If we confess our sins, he is faithful and just to forgive us our sins and to cleanse us from all unrighteousness." 1Jo 1:8-9

"By this we know we have come to know Him, if we keep His commandments." 1Jo 2:3

"Do not love the world or the things in the world. If anyone loves the world, the love of the Father is not in him." 1Jo 2:15

"For all that is in the world - the lust of the flesh and the lust of the eyes and pride of life - is not from the Father but is from the world." 1Jo 2:16

"They went out from us, but they were not of us; for if they had been of us, they would have continued with us. . ." 1Jo 2:19

"Whoever makes a practice of sinning is of the devil, for the devil has been sinning from the beginning. The reason the Son of God appeared was to destroy the works of the devil." 1Jo 3:8

"We love Him because He first loved us." 1Jo 4:19

"By this we know we love the children of God, when we love God and obey His commandments." 1Jo 5.2

"Whoever has the Son has life; whoever does not have the Son of God does not have life." 1Jo 5:12

"We know we are from God and the whole world lies in the power of the evil one." 1Jo 5:19

"And we know the Son of God has come and has given us understanding, so that we may know Him who is true; and we are in Him who is true, in His Son Jesus Christ. He is the true God and eternal life." 1Jo 5:20

"Little children, keep yourselves from idols." 1Jo 5:21

"To those who are called, beloved in God the Father and kept for Jesus Christ." Jud 1

"For certain people have crept in unnoticed who long ago were designated for this condemnation, ungodly people, who pervert the grace of our God into sensuality and deny our only Master and Lord, Jesus Christ." Jud 4

"Now to Him who is able to keep you from stumbling and to present you blameless before the presence of His glory with great joy, to the only God, our Savior, through Jesus Christ our Lord, be glory, majesty, dominion and authority, before all time and now and forever. Amen." Jud 24-25

"Worthy are you, our Lord and God, to receive glory and honor and power, for You created all things and by Your will they existed and were created." Rev 4:11

"Worthy are You to take the scroll and to open its seals, for You were slain and by Your blood You ransomed people for God from every tribe and language and people and nation and You have made them a kingdom and priests to our God and they shall reign on the earth." Rev 5:9-10

"They have conquered him by the blood of the Lamb and by the word of their testimony, for they loved not their lives even unto death." Rev 12:11

"All who dwell on earth will worship [the beast], everyone whose name has not been written before the foundation of the world in the book of life of the Lamb who was slain." Rev 13:8

"If anyone is to be taken captive, to captivity he goes; if anyone is to be slain with the sword, with the sword must he be slain." Rev 13:10

". . . Great and amazing are Your deeds, O Lord God the Almighty! Just and true are Your ways, O King of the nations! Who will not fear, O Lord and glorify Your name? For You alone are holy. All nations will come and worship You, for Your righteous acts have been revealed." Rev 15:3-4

". . . And the dwellers on earth whose names have not been written in the book of life from the foundation of the world will marvel to see the beast. . ." Rev 17:8

". . . Hallelujah! Salvation and glory and power belong to our God, for His judgments are true and just. . ." Rev 19:1-2

". . . The name by which He is called is The Word of God. . . From his mouth comes a sharp sword with which to strike down the nations and he will rule them with a rod of iron. . . On his robe and on his thigh he has a name written, King of kings and Lord of lords." Rev 19:13-16

"If anyone's name was not found written in the book of life, he was thrown into the lake of fire." Rev 20:15

"He who testifies to these things says, 'Surely I am coming soon.' Amen. Come, Lord Jesus! The grace of the Lord Jesus be with all the saints. Amen". Rev 22:20-21

Not Willing Any Should Perish

Recently, a discussion came up among friends whether it is right to claim a deceased mutual friend is in heaven with Christ or not. Actually, I tried to bring up the discussion and my friends became upset or outraged with me. Our mutual friend recently passed away and maybe I brought the subject up too soon but I had no choice as I believed God's justice was being defamed. For the sake of this story, we will call this friend Robert.

Robert received Christ in a church meeting when he was young. Several of my friends were there and some say they saw a radiance to his countenance, so they know he was saved. But it was not long before he was caught up in his old ways of stealing, alcohol abuse, sex and drugs. He lived his life this way, though every once in a while would come around to church to re-dedicate his life to the Lord. As time wore on, he found himself in and out of jail; soon he was fifty years old and soon he was dead.

One friend claimed he re-dedicated his life to Christ a couple weeks before he died, so they know he was saved. The fact of the matter is he died with his stash of drugs and the evidence is very slim he ever walked with the Lord - that he ever picked up his cross and followed Christ.

When the news came Robert was dead, most of our mutual friends posted their grief on social media along with their confidence he was now with Christ and the trials and hardships of his life are over. I hope this is true and it is possible he reconciled with God before he died. However, the evidence points in the other direction. While I would like to allow my friends the comfort of this delusion, I thought it was no minor sin to mock God. Thus I spoke up and thus my friends proceeded to rebuke me; one called me names, one ignored me altogether and several dismissed my arguments; ending our conversations about Robert.

One friend wrote: "Anyone who knows the effects of drugs on the brain, knows that when you start taking them, it damages the ability of the brain to develop properly. Robert lost his ability to reason properly when he started using drugs but I know he was saved. I was there when he asked Jesus to be his Savior. Yes, he rebelled. Haven't we all? There were times this rebellion was against God, but mostly he was running from himself. He always loved Jesus and had a soft spot for Him. He just wasn't able to walk the line. He literally wasn't capable of it from all the damage done to his brain from alcohol and drugs. But God never lets go of His own. He knows our hearts. Look how many times the Israelites wandered away from God and He always forgive them and drew them back to Himself, like the Good Shepherd He is. Why do you think God compares us to sheep? Because we ALL wander and have to be drawn back. And being callous, insensitive, and judgmental, are just as bad as Robert taking drugs. SIN IS SIN. But fortunately we serve a patient, loving, forgiving God. He is not waiting to strike us down. But you sure like to think He is. I have total peace and confidence that he is with Jesus. So shut your mouth for once and keep your callousness to yourself."

Regarding his struggles with drugs, one friend wrote, "I have had many talks with Robert, too, and he said he never lost faith, he just struggles with it but grows a bit closer to Him each time God gives him a 'time out.'"

Several members mentioned though Robert spent his life in sin and rebellion, he had a tender heart - he would give you the shirt off his back. Some blamed people in the church for his rebellion. It also occurred to some since he was raised in a Christian home, they can't help but believe that at the last he cried out to God - thus they know he was saved. Some brought up verses confirming those who believe are saved. One took this even further saying, "Salvation is God's gift, His to give, based upon His work not ours, so judgment comes only to those who despise God's work and establish their own code. We all are of faith and God honors the faith he has put within each of us (Eph 2:8,9) - to provide us a future and a hope (Jer 29:11)."

Most of my friends accused me of judging and told me only the one without sin should cast the first stone. One wrote, "Man looks at the outward appearance while God looks at the heart. God knew all of Robert's battles with the enemy and I believe Robert viewed surrendering to repentance as a form of weakness. Robert always liked viewing himself as the tough one, fight his own battles. He didn't realize that his kind of battles were all spiritual and only Jesus can fight those for us. I know God always wins in the end. I feel in my heart that the last word from his mouth was 'Jesus' and Robert will be there to greet us all into Heaven with his BIG smile as if to say, 'bet you all never expected me to beat you here.' I don't know about you but I'm gonna stomp on his foot after I hug him."

As if to try to wrap this all up, one of the group wrote, "If we make our best effort to LOVE the unlovely, to LOVE the undeserving, then the memories we can cling to will always be wonderful, because LOVE covers a multitude of sins. The greater the sin, the greater God's love and mercy will be to cover those sins. Robert was a sinner but guess what, we all are. Jesus loves us all, forgives us all and wants us in eternity with him when our time is done here."

It seemed to me my friends were not trying to be true to Scripture; they were attempting to salve their emotions. The Prophet Jeremiah warned us the heart is deceitful and desperately wicked (Jer 17:9) and the Apostle Paul warned us this does not change when we get saved (Rom 7). So we must be careful to walk after the Spirit and not after the flesh - or our personal comfort (Rom 8).

One evening several of us were together for dinner. I began the conversation with, "Isn't it interesting the modern Evangelical church tries to make salvation as easy as possible, while Jesus continually talked about how hard it is to be saved?" Every member present agreed with me and the conversation went along enforcing the Biblical theory it is hard to be saved. I determined not to talk about Robert - I just wanted to make my point against easy-believism, but by the time the conversation came to a close, he was there and it was agreed, among the rest, though he had lived his life in rebellion to God, God loved him and he was saved. One member ended the conversation with the words of Peter, "God is not willing any should perish."

In the Sermon on the Mount, Jesus warned us, "Judge not that you be not judged." [Mat 7:1] This is probably one of the most over-used verses in the Bible - often used to silence people from condemning sinful and evil actions. But Christ was talking about judging another man's relationship to God and/or condemning another for the sake of elevating ourself.

It is not hard to understand the sin of condemning a person whom God has chosen to save. We cannot judge someone not to be saved just because they do not meet our criteria of what a saved person looks like. But have we ever examined the opposite side of this coin? When we judge someone to be saved, when they might not be, we elevate a man whom God may have condemned, thus mocking God. In other words, when we say we know someone without a track record of following Christ is in heaven for the sake of bringing comfort to the hurting - even ourselves, we mock God who is judge of the living and the dead. Though our judging may have been with benevolent intent, the fruit is evil.

Mocking God is no small matter. I am wondering: When our Christian walk revolves around ourselves - God loves us; He has a wonderful plan for our lives and on and on - are we mocking God? When we say our faith is not a religion, it is a relationship; it is about including God in our life - are we mocking God? When we continually work for our own kingdom, although Jesus told us to pray for God's kingdom (Mat 6:10) and Isaiah told us to give God no rest on this matter (Isa 62) - are we mocking God? Are we following Christ, or is He tagging along? In the Sermon on the Mount, Jesus warned many professing Christians will not enter the kingdom of heaven (Mat 7). This gives me pause to often examine my walk with Christ (2Co 13:5).

Let us now examine the arguments of my friends:

Several friends mentioned they were there when Robert received Christ. One mentioned there was a radiance about him. This is wonderful - you were there for the event but how do we know from outside indications what goes on between God and man in the heart? If, after this event, we witness a life bearing fruit for Christ, we can be assured the person is truly saved. But if the next forty years are a life of rebellion - thieving, sex, alcohol abuse and drugs, we have no assurance the person is walking with the Lord, let alone saved - and, most likely not (Mat 7:16; Joh 15:1-6; 1Jo 2:19).

The classic model of a person saved in American Evangelicalism is reduced to an event: saying the sinner's prayer. It is generally accepted there is a repentance of sin and a change in the person's walk. But we treat these as optional because once the sinner's prayer is said, we declare this person is saved and cannot lose this salvation - mark the date down on your Gospel tract. But what say the Scriptures? There is no sinner's prayer.

In multiple passages we are told to believe and be saved. But what is believing since James tells us the demons believe and tremble (Jam 2:19) - and they are not saved? I think we can find a clue in Matthew chapter thirteen, in the parable of the Sower and the Seed given by Jesus. There are several places the seed landed and no fruit developed. However, there were two soils where the seed produced fruit: the good soil where the seed takes root - and these are the ones who are truly saved; and the stoney soil - they looked like they were saved at the beginning but they had no root and they withered. In today's terminology, they say the sinner's prayer but their fruit is short-lived. In this parable, believing is not an event; believing is the Gospel of Jesus Christ taking root in one's life.

The Apostle Paul tells us to work out our salvation with fear and trembling (Php 2:12). He is not recommending a salvation by works because in the very next verse he tells us it is God working through us. What he is talking about is our tendency to sin - even more, our determination to sin, as he talks about in the Book of Romans and especially chapter seven. We must be faithful in following Christ, knowing our God is holy and righteous and we are worthless sinners. This is a life, not an event.

Many people view Romans 10:9-10 - believing in your heart and confessing with your mouth - as an event. If you read this in context you will understand Paul is comparing a righteousness by following the law against a righteousness that comes from faith and he is talking about our lives, not an event.

Christ told us, in John chapter fifteen, He is the vine and we are the branches - referring to all the professing Christians. In verse six, He warns If we are not faithful in our walk we will wither and be tossed in the fire - the fires of Hell. Is Christ saying we can lose our salvation? Certainly not, however, not all professing Christians are saved (Mat 7:21). The Apostle John told us, "They went out from us, but they were not really of us; for if they had been they would have remained. But they left; making it clear they are not of us." [1Jo 2:19] In other words, it is not the sinner's prayer that saves; it is only those who remain to the end who were saved in the first place. Salvation is not found in an event; it is a daily walk.

What about the re-dedications? Even if Robert's walk was not faithful - and even rebellious - don't his multiple re-dedications at least indicate he "had a soft spot for Jesus," as one of the friends put it? I talked to Robert on at least a couple occasions, if not several, about this matter. He told me he wanted to make sure he had fire insurance. He had been raised on this and was firmly convinced of the matter. I, too, was raised on this and would try to get people to say the sinner's prayer - if only to make sure they had fire insurance. But the Lord brought me out of this theology decades ago and I warned him against this as there is no fire insurance according to the Scriptures.

Robert was not to be convinced - he wanted his life of rebellion but he wanted assurance there were no eternal consequences - he wanted fire insurance. The Bible tells us obedience is better than sacrifice - or re-dedication, if you will - but rebellion is a great sin (1Sa 15:22-23). The Apostle Peter told us Christ died for us so that we might die to sin and live for righteousness, or obedience (2Pe 2:24). Scripture is clear, salvation is not found in an event nor is it found in a series of events. It is found only in a life of obedience to the Gospel of Jesus Christ (Joh 3:36; 15:1-6; 1Jo 2:3).

Do we think it is a small matter to declare someone saved who is not? to assure them of salvation if they were sincere? to give them the Illusion of fire insurance a cheap escape from Hell if they say the sinners prayer? Do we think God will not hold us accountable for deceiving people to think they were saved because our intention was to get someone saved?

During our exchange of emails, some of our mutual friends resorted to blame. Several blamed his addiction to drugs and one blamed people from the church. The Apostle Paul makes clear in Romans chapter one God has revealed Himself to all men - so that no man is without excuse. To blame other professing Christians for Robert's falling away is without Scriptural support. We blame to escape responsibility or to remove responsibility from where it belongs. But the Scripture is clear - no man is without excuse.

Can someone be so lost to drugs so that when they get saved they are powerless to follow Christ? Christ commanded us to daily take up our cross and follow Him and those unwilling to do so are not worthy of Him (Mat 10:38; 16:24). Every Christian has their cross to bear, some crosses are heavier than others. Drugs are a cruel master but the professing Christian must choose to continue to follow the old master or follow Christ. No matter how severe the addiction, every use of drugs boils down to a choice - nobody is forced to do it. The Apostle Paul tells us in Romans chapter six, we are slaves to the one we choose to obey. Remember the parable of the Sower and the Seed: some seed falls on the rocky soil, it blossoms but there is no root, so it withers and dies. The only reason Robert was powerless to obey Christ was because he had no root. We cannot blame drugs nor can we blame other professing Christians who let him down.

The Apostle Paul wrote when we are saved we are a new creation - the old is gone (2Co 5:17). Instead of accepting this truth, we find a multitude of professing Christians struggling to find identity within their church sponsored recovery group.

Is the arm of the Lord too short to save (Isa 59:1)? Are drugs too much for Christ to overcome? I remember when God called me - I was in the gutter, a hopeless drunk. He called me to follow Him and I left the drunken life behind. Isaiah wrote our sins have separated us from God and hidden His face (Isa 59:2). Christ told people immersed in sinful lives to go and sin no more (Joh 8:11). We hear of some of the painful withdrawals of addicts who appear to have chosen Christ only to return to their lives of debauchery. Is this God's fault - is He powerless? Or is the real problem the professing Christian prefers his old master - and was never saved at all?

There are those who find victory in their struggles when they determine to follow Christ.

If one were to summarize the first chapter of the Book of James, it would be this: In your trials, do not sin. One member of our group claimed Robert never lost faith during these trials - trials being his bondage to drugs, sex and alcohol abuse. Clinging to a life of sin is not a trial - it is rebellion, just as Paul described it in Romans chapter one. Every admonishment in Scripture to persevere in the faith warns us to follow Christ - not the world and not the flesh. The Apostle John wrote if we say we have fellowship with - or faith in - Christ but continue in our sin, we are lying (1Jo 1:6). We cannot follow Christ and follow darkness (Mat 6:24; Joh 3:19).

In Romans chapter six, Paul asked two questions: 1) Shall we go on sinning that grace may increase?; and 2) Shall we sin because we are not under the law but under grace? The answer to both is "by no means" (or "God forbid") - we have died to sin and are slaves to whom we choose to obey. If we choose to obey righteousness, our lives will lead to holiness - not to debauchery. For the wages of sin is death...

Is God a God of mercy? The Bible tells us over and over this is true. However, we know from Scripture salvation is not universal. In Romans chapter nine, the Apostle Paul made clear God has mercy on those He has chosen. So to whom is this mercy directed? "These are the ones I look on with favor: those who are humble and contrite in spirit, and who tremble at my word." [Isa 66:2]. This verse describes those who follow Christ.

Several friends commented Robert "had a tender heart - he would give you the shirt off his back." They are confusing this with a contrite spirit. The Bible differentiates between the humble and those living a life of sin (Psa 18:27; 147:6; Pro 3:33-35; Jam 4:6; 1Pe 5:5). The famous verse, 2Chronicles 7:14, tells us the humble will turn away from sin. If we continue in sin, we are neither contrite nor humble and there is no mercy for us (Heb 10).

So, what is faith? The writer of the Book of Hebrews told us faith is the assurance of things hoped for, the conviction of things not seen (Heb 11:1). Then he continued his description of faith by listing the acts of obedience of well-known predecessors in the faith.

In the second chapter of James, there is a comparison of three examples of faith: the faith of Abraham, the father of Israel; the faith of Rahab, the prostitute; and the faith of demons.

Because of his faith, Abraham acted in obedience to God's commands, including leaving the comfort of his home to live in tents and laying his son on the altar as a sacrifice to God. Not many of us can fully understand living a life with nothing but God - to have no permanent residence and the willingness to give a long-hoped-for son back to God. God was faithful and honored Abraham's obedience not only by restoring his son but by bringing the Salvation of mankind through his seed.

Rahab was a prostitute. She heard of the power of Israel's God and believed Jericho was destined to destruction. Some might call this "faith." But this knowledge or fear was not faith and she was not the only one who was afraid. However, she was the only one who believed in the God of Israel as the only true God and she acted on this belief. She hid the spies and lied to the authorities - at the risk of her life. God blessed her faith which was proven by her actions. Not only was her family rescued from destruction but God placed her in the line of David and our Redeemer, Jesus Christ. Her faith was not produced by works, or a sinless life, but her faith produced works that led to life.

According to modern Christian thought, Rahab could have exercised her faith by turning the spies in to the authorities. Romans 13:1 tells us to be subject to our governing authorities. Most professing Christians I talk to interpret the first seven verses of Romans thirteen through the lens of the first clause of the first verse. Forgotten, or ignored, are Paul's admonishments that governments are instituted to do good, bless those who do good and restrain evil. This misinterpretation of this passage has given many a professing Christians shelter from having to stand against the evil in their day - they place man as the highest authority. But Peter and John stood firm, stating "we must obey God rather than man" (Act 4:19; 5:29). Because God instituted all government, He is the highest authority (Dan 2:20-12). Therefore, we must stand firm for God's truth even when governments promote evil.

Abraham and Rahab had a saving faith - as did the list of those mentioned in Hebrews eleven. Their faith was a saving faith because they were not afraid to act on their faith - to live out obedience to the glory of God.

The third faith James demonstrates (actually the first in order) is the faith of demons. Demons believe because they know - they have seen God. Yet they cannot be saved, so their faith is not a saving faith. When we say we have faith yet fail to live in obedience, not only does John say we are liars but we demonstrate the faith of demons and we cannot be saved. The Apostle James wrote "I will show you my faith by my works ... faith without works is dead." [Jam 2:14-26] Be doers of the Word and not hearers only (Jam 1:22).

The easy-believism faith says, "Come. Say the sinner's prayer and you will be saved. Nothing is required because salvation is not of works. Once you are saved, you can never lose your salvation because God loves you. No matter how far you fall, God loves you and no one slips out of His hands." I thought it was very ironic one of the friends wrote in defense of Robert, "So judgment comes only to those who despise God's work and establish their own code." Not only was Robert's rebellion a despising of God's work, it was a living out of his own code. However, I think a more important point is that we mock God - or despise His work - and establish our own code when we relegate salvation to an event - a sinner's prayer - and ignore or deny salvation is lived out in a life of obedience to God. Salvation is found only by abiding in Christ - this is the fruit of faith in Christ.

Sure, we all know the verse that says salvation is by grace and not of works, lest any man boast in himself (Eph 2:8-9). But we ignore the very next verse which clearly says our salvation, or faith, produces works that God prepared in advance for us - "that we should walk in them."

The Bible makes clear those who preach easy-believism are not preaching the Gospel of Jesus Christ. Many a professing Christian are on their way to hell because they are living for their own kingdom and not for the kingdom of heaven. They believe they can live any way they please because they are not saved by works. They believe once they say the sinner's prayer they have their fire insurance locked in. Taking up their cross daily consists of being stuck in traffic, suffering through a job they despise or not getting paid enough for the work they do. Lost to them is the ideal of abiding in Christ, denying themselves and standing up for God's truth in the midst of an evil generation - fearing God, not man.

Consider these words of Jesus: "Enter by the narrow gate for the wide gate is easy and leads to destruction and those who enter are many. But the narrow gate is hard and few will find it but it leads to life." [Mat 7:13-14] I was taught the narrow gate was following Christ and the wide gate was following the world. The more I read this passage the more I am convinced Christ is speaking of the faith. The wide gate is not the world because the world is content to wander ignoring the path to God. The wide gate is the way of the majority of professing Christians - they enter the easy way; the way to destruction. Those who enter the narrow gate are those who are willing to follow Christ.

If we deny ourselves and take up our cross to follow Christ, the Apostle Paul assured us Christ will bring this work to completion (Php 1:6). Our salvation does not consist of an event or a prayer - it is a life lived for Christ.

Going back to the conversation with friends at the dinner table, one member summed up Robert's salvation with "God is not willing any should perish." Great verse but one of the most wrongly used verses.

A basic rule for interpreting Scripture is to look at it within the context of the passage around it. When looking at the context of this clause we see Peter is talking to the elect - make your calling and election sure (1:10). In the first verse of chapter three, Peter references his first epistle to these same people and in that epistle he addresses them as the elect at the very start. Then we look at chapter two of 2Peter, it is a list of people, throughout all time that God is not willing to save and has destined to destruction. In chapter three, Peter said the ungodly will be damned (3:7).

So, at this point we know there are exceptions to "God is not willing any should perish." Then, in the ninth verse, where Peter wrote "God is not willing any should perish," he prefaced it with, "He is longsuffering toward us" - us, the elect - then he continued, "not willing that any should perish." So, if we take this verse in context, Peter is talking to and about the elect when he wrote "God is not willing any should perish." He is not talking about those in rebellion to Him - regardless whether they said the sinner's prayer or whether they claimed to be saved.

After we have examined a verse within the context of the passage, we should compare it according to what the rest of Scripture has to say about. If we think God is not willing any person should perish, this is the same God who rejected an entire generation of Israelites, leaving them to die in the desert. This is the same God who told Jeremiah on four different occasions not to pray for his generation of Israelites. In Matthew chapter thirteen,

Jesus explained He spoke in parables lest the people hearing understand and believe. And, this same Jesus made it clear He only prayed for those who are His and not the people of the world (Joh 17:9).

When Jesus explained to the disciples it is difficult for the rich to enter the kingdom of heaven, they had a hard time understanding (Mat 19:16-30). Because just like many modern professing Christians, they believed wealth was a sign of God's blessing. Jesus explained we must deny ourselves and in John chapter fifteen He said we must abide in Him in order to produce fruit; otherwise we perish - by fire. Many who believe they are saved are not. Think about this because Jesus said so in Matthew 7:21. Think about the Apostle Paul's warning to examine ourselves to see if we are in the faith (2Co 13:5).

In John 2:23-25, many claimed to believe but Christ had no confidence in them because He knows the heart of man - in other words, they were not saved. In John chapter 6, speaking to believers, Jesus made His testimony hard to understand and people were stumbling over what He was saying. He told them they cannot come to Him unless the Father draws them. In John chapter eight, Jesus told believers they will stumble over the truth unless they abide in Christ and even then, they stumbled over what He said. And I won't get into Romans chapter nine where Paul claims some are created for destruction. So, unlike modern easy-believism which boils salvation down to a recitation of the sinner's prayer, Jesus tells us the truth is hidden from those not chosen; we can only come to faith in Christ if the Father draws us; and if we do not produce fruit, we will perish. So, we see from Scripture God qualifies those He is not willing should perish.

Nothing in this story is meant to demean or condemn my friend, Robert. My heart grieves that he might be going to hell. That I have analyzed this scenario at all is to convince us to examine our faith because I firmly believe we have mocked God by claiming Robert to be in heaven. Now, it just might be he cried out to God at the end, but we don't know this to be true and the evidence is against it when we examine what the Scriptures declare to be a life that is saved. If we err, we must err on the side of honoring God - to avoid mocking Him if there is any doubt.

Now, please don't misunderstand what I am trying to get across. I am not claiming we must be perfect to be saved and I am no super Christian, myself. I sin daily; I negligently mock God and take His ways and His Word frivolously; I know my heart is full of evil and I bear little fruit. I plead with God daily not to abandon me to my sin. All I can do is confess my sin and ask God to lead me and help me follow.

This is my cross: rejecting my sin nature's constant determination to sin. My concern and the only reason I write this is to exhort myself and anyone who reads this to look at our lives and look at our walk with Christ so the seed within us will take root and we will be diligent to bring Him honor by bearing fruit.

The Apostle Paul told us to rightly divide the Word of Truth (2Ti 2:15). Do we think it is no small matter to fail in this if our intention is to get someone saved? or to bring comfort to the bereaved? Do we think God will not hold us accountable because our intentions were good - in our own eyes? (see Jer 17:9).

If we are in grief, let us bear this trial without sinning knowing God will confirm us to the end (1Co 1:8).

Keep the faith.

Freewill vs John 3:16

Probably the most memorized Scripture in the Bible is John 3:16: "For God so loved the world, He gave His only begotten Son, so that whoever believes in Him should not perish but have everlasting life." Many Christians treat this Scripture as a stand alone verse promoting man's freewill and the idea God loves everyone and they neglect to look at the verse in context with the conversation and other Scripture.

The context of this verse is this: the Pharisee Nicodemus was having a conversation with Christ Jesus. The Jews believed the Messiah would come and save them from an Roman oppression. Jesus told him He had come for more than the Jews - He had come for the world.

Who is the world? It is problematic to interpret John 3:16 to mean Christ died for the sins of the whole world. Certainly, most Christians do not believe in universal salvation – the idea that all men are saved. However, when challenged to compare this verse between the opposing views of universal salvation and God's predestination of the elect - which is hard for most modern, American Christians to accept, many will settle for the interpretation Christ died for the sins of the whole world but only those who believe are saved. And, in the face of competing doctrines, this interpretation can appear to be safe – and less controversial – but it is wrong.

Having been raised on easy-believism, I was in this camp. However, the more I read and studied the Scriptures, the more the doctrines of the elect and predestination jumped out at me. You might think I was studying these doctrines while armed with commentaries but I was not and had read no books. In fact, all I had was a Scofield Study Bible and I read it over and over again and studied and studied the footnotes. But the more I read Scripture and the more I studied, the more I disagreed with Scofield's notes.

For those who know of Scofield's works, you know he is not in agreement with the Reformed view of election or predestination. He is one of the modern day authors of freewill, choice and easy-believism. My experience demonstrates when God decides to give wisdom, no author's notes are going to get in the way.

So when this verse says "so loved the world," either Christ died for everyone's sin and God is looking at the world as forgiven, or there must be some exclusions to the definition of the word "world." If there are some exclusions, then there are some people Christ did not die for. However, this must be true, because even within the verse when Christ said, "whoever believes in Him should not perish but have everlasting life" He qualified someone must believe to be saved and therefore implied some cannot be saved. At minimum, whoever does not believe is summarily excluded from salvation. I think further study will demonstrate they are excluded from "so loved the world" as well.

Many are the claims John 3:16 means God loves the whole world and these same people often cite Romans 5:8, "God demonstrates His love for us in that while we were sinners, Christ died for us." The problem with this view it is taking both verses out of context: John 3:16, we will continue to examine and Romans 5:8 is talking about the elect the ones God chose to save; it is not referring to all sinners.

Men wiser than I have concluded or at least have concluded in selected writings (I don't know if they later changed their minds) that God loves all sinners. Among these are John Calvin and John MacArthur. If I remember correctly, a couple reasons are 1) God loves all His creation; and 2) God extends His offer of salvation to all - even to those who are not chosen. Though I agree with their premise I cannot reach the same conclusion - that God loves all sinners. For as I read and study Scripture, I agree God loves all His creation, in the general sense. It is understandable that He would because He made everything and it is His (Col 1:16). However, I think it is possible to love all collectively, yet not love all individually. As for extending His offer of salvation to all, can the reason be to hold every man accountable rather than being an expression of His love?

When facing the question whether God loves those not chosen, here is what I wrestle with: The Apostle John, quoting the Prophet Isaiah, wrote God had blinded the peoples eyes and hardened their hearts - so they could not see and understand the Gospel and, correspondingly, God would not save them (Joh 12:40). To keep them from seeing and understanding the truth is not a demonstration of love. On one occasion, rejoicing in the Holy Spirit, Christ praised the Father for hiding the truth from the wise and learned and revealing it to the few who were chosen (Luk 10:21). Why would Christ be thankful and rejoicing the truth was hidden from so many if He loved them?

Then we look at the controversial passage, written by the Apostle Paul, in Romans chapter nine. Paul claimed God chose some for life and some for death and, according to what He wrote to the Ephesians, God make this selection - or election - before He created the world (Eph 1:4). If He chose some for eternal destruction, how is this love? Nonetheless, even in this passage, Paul declared the grace, mercy and infinite love of God when he wrote, "What if God desiring to show His wrath and great power, endured patiently those created for destruction, in order to demonstrate His great love and mercy to those who were chosen beforehand - before creation?" [Rom 9:22-23, paraphrased]. This is love and God's love is lavished upon the chosen but demonstrated in no way toward those who were not written in the Book of Life before the creation of the world (see Rev 13:8; 17:8).

It is clear in Scripture God does not love evil and there are many Scriptures listing the evil men God hates. Going back to Romans chapter nine, God said He loved Jacob and hated Esau - even before they were born; before they had done good or evil. Leviticus 20:23 tells us God told the Israelites He abhors the nations He will drive out before them - He did not love the people there.

Psalm 2 tells us God mocks and despises the nations of the world because of their rebellion. Psalm 5:5 tells us God hates all who do iniquity. Psalm 11:5 tells us God hates those who love violence. Psalm 15:4 tells us God despises a vile person. Proverbs 6:16-19 tells us seven things the Lord hates and the people who do these. Three times in the Book of Jeremiah (7:16; 11:14; 14:11) God hated the Israelites so much Jeremiah was commanded not to pray for them. Hosea 9:15 tells us God hated the children of Ephraim because of their wicked deeds. Romans chapter 1 tells us how God gave the rebellious over to their sin and 2Peter chapter two continues this list, mentioning false teachers, partiers and others whom God has already condemned. The idea that God loves the sinner but hates the sin is not to be found anywhere in Scripture. The sin and the sinner are both hated by God and anywhere the Bible mentions God extending His love toward sinners has to do with God's elect - His chosen. In this, He demonstrates His great mercy, as no man deserves to be chosen by God.

There are three Scriptures I believe are key when considering who Jesus was referring to when He said, "God so loved the world."

The first Scripture is Mark 10:45. In this verse, Jesus said He came to give His life as a ransom for many. The first thing to consider in this is the ransom: A ransom is paid to redeem someone who belongs to you – it is not generic or universal. If Christ came to save all men, He failed - but God does not fail. The second thing to consider, in this passage, is the "many." Christ did not claim to ransom "all" or everyone in the world nor did he ever say He was going to die for everyone's sin.

The second Scripture to consider is Revelation 5:9. The praise in this verse is, "by Your blood You ransomed people for God from every tribe and language and people and nation." Here again is the concept of a ransom and the ransom is for people from the whole world – every portion of the world but not everyone in the world. This again defines the "many."

The third Scripture to consider is Isaiah chapter 53. In verse 6, Isaiah wrote, "the Lord has laid on Him the iniquity of us all." Later in the chapter, in verses 11 and 12, it is clarified who is the "all." In these two verses, the prophet reveals from his sufferings, the Messiah, will "make many to be accounted righteous, and He shall bear their iniquities." Here again, is the "many" - the ones who will "be accounted righteous" and it is clear it is for their iniquities He suffered. Three times the "many" are referenced in these two verses and the third time it is reinforced whose sin Christ bore on the cross – "He bore the sin of many."

These three passages are key to identifying who Christ died for – and the quantity. Did Christ ransom the entire world from sin, or the many? And, if the many, who are they? John 1:9-13 and 6:44, 65 help us to understand who are the many. In these verses we find those who receive Christ are drawn by the Father and are saved by the will of God, not by the will of man. We are not saved because of our choice but because of God's choice (Joh 1:13) and Christ confirmed this when He said no one comes to Him unless the Father draw him (Joh 6:44).

We see from this examination two platitudes we have been taught are not true. We like to think of God as love but we see from Scripture 1) He does not hate the sin but love the sinner - He hates those He has not chosen; and 2) Christ did not die for everyone in the world - He died for those He chose from before the foundation of the world.

Going back to John 3, what does this chapter say about freewill? In the third verse of John chapter three, Jesus made clear man cannot be saved by his own choice or freewill. He said if a man is not born again, he cannot see the kingdom of God.

Let's talk about being born and being born again: A man and woman may choose to have a child but they cannot choose the soul who will be born to them. God uses their willingness and, in other cases, their unwillingness to bring to life the soul He chooses. The person born is not born of his own choice, for no one chooses to be born. So, too, to be born again is not by man's choice. As the Apostle John wrote in the first chapter, those who receive Christ and believe in His name are born not by the will of man but by God's will (Joh 1:12-13). There is nothing in the Book of John and especially in this third chapter that would lend itself to the doctrine of man coming to salvation of his own freewill.

In the fifth chapter of John, Christ said He gives life to whomever He wills (Joh 5:21). He did not say it was to those who choose Him but to those He chooses or wills and in John 15:16 He said, "You did not choose Me but I chose you." To further refute mans' ability to come to Him, He said, "No one can come to Me unless the Father draws him." [Joh 6:44] and no one can come to Christ unless granted or allowed by the Father (Joh 6:65). This backs up what He said just a few verses earlier, the only ones who can receive Him are those the Father has given Him (Joh 6:37). The Apostle Paul wrote God's choosing does not depend upon our will or effort (Rom 9:16). In this chapter, Paul cites God's authority as being the potter over the clay (see also Isa 29:16; 64:8; Jer 18). This is a hard thing to accept - that we are not in control of our own salvation.

Even the Jews, in their limited view of redemption, knew not all children of Abraham were saved (Mat 22:34-40; Luk 10:25-28). Nicodemus was a learned man of the Pharisees. To Nicodemus, salvation was tied to obedience of the law and, if one was obedient to the law, to some degree he could claim control over his salvation. This is how legalism or salvation by works develops: It grows from the desire to be in control.

Nicodemus had a hard time with the concept being born again to be an act of God alone - not of man. This is why he asked Christ how a man can be born when he is old or how can he reenter the womb - both acts are impossible, if not absurd. He had come to inquire of Christ - viewing Him as a higher authority - but he wanted to retain control - both of this conversation and his salvation.

Christ's answer was direct: to be saved, man must be born again, but this act is of God alone and it is impossible for man to see or understand how and why the Holy Spirit acts (Joh 3:5-8). As the Apostle Paul wrote in the first chapter of Ephesians, those who believe were chosen according to the purpose of

God's will (Eph 1:4-5, 11). This is also why, when the disciples could not understand why it was hard for the wealthy to be saved, Jesus said with God all things are possible (Mat 19:23-26). We do not understand the ways of God.

Jesus said if you sin you are a slave to sin (Joh 8:34) and the Apostle Paul affirmed this, stating we are slaves to the one we obey (Rom 6:16). If you are a slave to sin, how can you choose God? In Romans chapter eight, the Apostle Paul wrote if we are in the flesh, we are hostile to God and cannot please Him - or choose Him (Rom 8:5-8). To modify a quote from Charles Spurgeon, a man's will is either led captive by sin or is held in the blessed bonds of grace.

Paul said we are saved by God's grace alone; not by works or anything else we can do – we cannot even "make a decision" – lest any man should boast (Ep 2:8-9). Our only participation in the Gospel of Salvation is that of recipient. We can only receive it – and even this is by the grace of God because the Bible is clear there is NO one who seeks after God (Psa 14:1-3; Isa 53:6 ; Rom 3:10-11) because the natural bent of our hearts is rebellion toward God.

When men asked Jesus what they must do to be doing the work of God, He turned the whole question around. He said to believe in the One whom He has sent - but He said this is God's work; not mans' (Joh 6:28-29). We know from context this is what He meant because he went on to say, "All the Father gives Me will come to Me" [verse 37] and "No one can come to Me unless the Father draws him [verse 44] and, just as He told Nicodemus in John 3:5-8, "it is the Spirit who gives life, the flesh is no help at all." [Joh 6:63]. In other words, we are powerless to choose God - it is God who chooses us.

So, we see Christ never intended John 3:16 to support the idea of choosing God of our own freewill. Modern American Evangelicals will pound on this idea while begging and pleading the lost sinner to "give his heart to

Jesus" - which, by the way is found nowhere in Scripture. Nor do we see in Scripture, Jesus begging or pleading with the masses. He spoke the words of His Father and did what He saw His Father doing (Joh 5:19; 12:49). This is our model and it is the essence of our role in the Great Commission (Mat 28:18-20). We do not beg and plead: we teach all nations and baptize the believers. We profess and teach the truth and wait upon God, who brings those He has given to His Son.

Therefore, it is important to interpret John 3:16 in the context of Scripture and not in the context of man's sovereignty or freewill. The Scriptures proclaim God's sovereignty. To use John 3:16 to promote choice or freewill or to promote the premise God loves everyone in the world - or hates the sin but loves the sinner - is a serious doctrinal error.

Keep the faith.

May this book be helpful in encouraging sound doctrine and may you continue to consider, meditate upon and memorize the verses in this book. Whether you come to the same conclusions as I or not, may your theology be grounded in the whole of Scripture - rightly dividing the Word of Truth and not a reliance upon platitudes, theories or theologies you were taught. Don't be careless - enter by the narrow way. May we always remember the purpose of our walk with Christ is to give all glory to God. Amen.

God is ProLife

www.ingramcontent.com/pod-product-compliance
Lightning Source LLC
Chambersburg PA
CBHW071304040426
42444CB00009B/1865